Lenovo Laptop Bible

A User-Friendly Approach to Advanced Technology

Tech Trends

TABLE OF CONTENTS

Lenovo Laptop Bible

Introduction to Lenovo Laptops: A Legacy of Innovation

Lenovo has steadily carved its niche as a global leader in the laptop industry through a journey marked by strategic acquisitions, technological advancements, and an unwavering commitment to quality. The company's ascent to becoming a household name in personal computing began long before it was recognized globally under the "Lenovo" brand, with roots tracing back to the late 20th century. Today, Lenovo's laptops are synonymous with reliability, cutting-edge design, and user-centric innovations.

Overview of Lenovo's Journey in the Laptop Industry

Lenovo's laptop story begins in 1984 when the company was founded as "Legend" in Beijing, China, with an initial focus on distributing IBM computers in China. The first significant breakthrough came in 1990 when the company launched its first computer, marking the start of its own product line. During the 1990s, Lenovo (still operating under the Legend brand) focused on building its presence in the Chinese market.

The turning point came in 2005, when Lenovo acquired IBM's Personal Computing Division, including the ThinkPad line. This move instantly transformed Lenovo into a global player, inheriting IBM's reputation for quality and innovation in the corporate and business laptop market. The acquisition was strategic not only because of the ThinkPad's iconic status but also for the advanced technologies Lenovo could now tap into, including IBM's research and development in mobile computing. The

ThinkPad series would later become a symbol of Lenovo's engineering excellence.

Key Milestones and Innovations Over the Years

Lenovo's journey in laptops is marked by several key innovations and strategic developments that positioned it as a market leader:

1. **2005: Acquisition of IBM's ThinkPad**
   The acquisition of IBM's ThinkPad line is one of Lenovo's most significant milestones. ThinkPad was already considered a gold standard for business laptops due to its durability, security, and performance. Lenovo continued to build on these strengths, introducing enhanced models that kept the core values of the ThinkPad brand intact while adding more modern features. Under Lenovo's stewardship, the ThinkPad line introduced features like the **TrackPoint**, the **ThinkShutter** camera privacy cover, and

continued refining the **UltraNav** touchpad system.

2. **2008: Introduction of the IdeaPad Series**

   Lenovo didn't limit itself to the business market; it expanded into the consumer market with the introduction of the **IdeaPad** series. These laptops were designed to appeal to a broader audience, focusing on multimedia, entertainment, and home computing. The IdeaPad series brought a fresh design language compared to the ThinkPad's industrial look, and it was also more affordable, catering to students, families, and casual users. This move diversified Lenovo's portfolio and helped capture a larger share of the global market.

3. **2012: Launch of the Yoga Series**

   Lenovo redefined laptop flexibility with the **Yoga** series, introducing the world to 2-in-1 convertible laptops. The Yoga's 360-degree hinge allowed users to switch between laptop, tent, stand, and tablet modes, meeting the demand for versatile devices that could handle both work and leisure tasks. This innovation paved the way for hybrid laptops, which are now a staple in the market. The Yoga series continues to be a leader in this segment, evolving with each generation to include features like high-resolution displays, touchscreens, and better battery life.

4. **2014: Acquisition of Motorola Mobility** While primarily known for laptops, Lenovo's acquisition of **Motorola Mobility** was a strategic move to expand its footprint in mobile computing. Although this acquisition focused more on smartphones, it also allowed Lenovo to integrate mobile technology innovations into its laptops, like better connectivity and power efficiency. This deal underscored Lenovo's intention to be a major player across all computing devices, not just PCs.

5. **2017: Introduction of the Legion Gaming Line**

Lenovo's entry into gaming laptops with the **Legion** brand represented another major milestone. Targeting the booming gaming market, Lenovo designed high-performance laptops with top-tier specs such as **NVIDIA GeForce GPUs**, high-refresh-rate displays, and sophisticated cooling systems to handle the demanding requirements of modern gaming. The Legion series has gained traction among gamers, competing against established gaming brands like Alienware and Razer.

6. **2018: The First Foldable PC**
   Lenovo once again demonstrated its commitment to innovation by unveiling the world's first foldable laptop, the **ThinkPad X1 Fold**, in 2018. This device featured a folding OLED screen, combining the portability of a tablet with the functionality of a laptop. The ThinkPad X1 Fold showcased Lenovo's ability to push the boundaries of conventional laptop design and explore

new form factors that align with the future of personal computing.

7. **2022: AI-Powered Laptops**
With the rise of artificial intelligence, Lenovo began integrating AI-driven features into its laptops, enhancing productivity and user experience. Laptops like the **Yoga Slim 7i Pro** and **ThinkPad X1 Carbon** now come equipped with AI capabilities such as intelligent cooling, adaptive screen brightness, and noise-cancelling microphones, all powered by Lenovo's proprietary AI engine. These advancements help to optimise performance, prolong battery life, and improve the overall user experience.

8. **Sustainability and Green Innovations**
Lenovo has also committed to sustainable practices in recent years. The company's **ThinkPad X1** laptops, for example, are built with a focus on reducing environmental impact. Lenovo uses recycled materials in its laptops,

implements energy-efficient manufacturing processes, and is actively reducing its carbon footprint across its supply chain. The company's goal of becoming carbon-neutral by 2050 further reinforces its leadership in this area.

9. **2024: Launch of the Yoga Pro 9i and Legion 7i**

   Most recently, Lenovo introduced the **Yoga Pro 9i** and **Legion 7i**, featuring the latest Intel Core Ultra processors and AI-powered features. These new laptops come equipped with advanced thermal management, gaming-ready GPUs, and longer battery life, solidifying Lenovo's place in both the creative and gaming markets. These models are prime examples of Lenovo's focus on blending AI-driven technology with user-centric designs, keeping up with the latest trends while setting new standards.

Choosing the Right Lenovo Laptop: A Comprehensive Buying Guide

Lenovo offers a diverse range of laptops, catering to various needs—from business professionals to gamers, creatives, and everyday users. With multiple series such as Yoga, ThinkBook, Legion, IdeaPad, and ThinkPad, each Lenovo laptop is tailored for different use cases and preferences. Understanding the key differences between these models and identifying which factors matter most can help you make the right choice based on your specific needs.

Breakdown of Different Lenovo Laptop Series

1. Yoga Series

The Yoga line is designed for users seeking flexibility and versatility in their devices. These laptops are convertible, meaning they can be used in multiple modes: laptop, tent, stand, and tablet. This makes them ideal for individuals who want a device that can handle various tasks—work, creativity, and entertainment—all in one. The Yoga series often features touchscreen displays, stylus support, and vibrant high-resolution screens.

- **Key Features**:
    - 2-in-1 convertible design.
    - Premium build quality with sleek aluminium chassis.
    - High-resolution touchscreen displays with HDR support.

- o Support for digital styluses, ideal for artists and designers.
- **Target Audience**:
    - o Creatives, artists, and designers who need a flexible machine.
    - o Professionals who want the convenience of a tablet for presentations or note-taking.
    - o Users looking for a premium, versatile device for both work and leisure.

2. ThinkBook Series

The ThinkBook series combines the performance and reliability of a business laptop with modern design elements that appeal to younger professionals and small businesses. These laptops offer a balance between affordability and functionality, making them ideal for business users who require performance without the bulk or high price tags of traditional business laptops.

- **Key Features**:

- Thin and lightweight design with an emphasis on portability.
- Strong security features, including fingerprint readers and webcam privacy shutters.
- Business-oriented software and hardware, including powerful processors and ample connectivity options.

- **Target Audience**:
  - Entrepreneurs, small business owners, and young professionals.
  - Users looking for a combination of work-focused features and portability.
  - Individuals seeking a cost-effective business laptop without compromising on essential functions.

3. Legion Series

The Legion line is specifically designed for gaming and high-performance tasks. These laptops are equipped with the latest CPUs and

GPUs, making them perfect for gamers and creators who demand high computing power. The Legion series includes features like enhanced cooling systems, RGB backlighting, and high-refresh-rate displays to ensure a smooth gaming experience.

- **Key Features**:
    - Powerful CPUs and discrete NVIDIA GeForce RTX graphics.
    - Advanced cooling systems for sustained performance during intensive gaming or creative work.
    - High-refresh-rate displays (up to 240Hz) for fluid and responsive gaming visuals.
    - RGB keyboard backlighting and customizable gaming profiles.
- **Target Audience**:
    - Gamers who need the best performance for modern games.
    - Creatives working with 3D rendering, video editing, and other resource-intensive applications.

○ Users who require a high-performance machine for multitasking and demanding tasks.

4. ThinkPad Series

ThinkPads are Lenovo's flagship business laptops, known for their robust build quality, excellent keyboards, and enterprise-level security. The ThinkPad line has become synonymous with durability and reliability, making it the go-to choice for corporate environments and professionals who need a laptop that can withstand heavy daily use.

- **Key Features**:
    - ○ Excellent build quality with MIL-STD tested durability.
    - ○ Best-in-class keyboards, featuring Lenovo's iconic TrackPoint.
    - ○ Enterprise-grade security features, including encrypted drives, biometric authentication, and a wide range of ports.

- ○ Long battery life and optional LTE connectivity for working on the go.
- **Target Audience**:
  - ○ Corporate professionals, executives, and IT departments looking for reliable business laptops.
  - ○ Travellers who need a durable laptop with long battery life and reliable connectivity.
  - ○ Users who prioritise security and performance in their daily computing needs.

5. IdeaPad Series

IdeaPads are designed for casual users, students, and families. These laptops focus on providing a good balance of performance and price, with a wide range of configurations available to suit different budgets. While not as feature-rich as ThinkPads or Legion laptops, IdeaPads still offer solid performance for everyday computing tasks such as web browsing, media consumption, and light productivity.

- **Key Features**:
  - Affordable pricing with a variety of configurations.
  - Balanced performance for general computing tasks.
  - Lightweight designs, making them easy to carry around.
  - Decent battery life for casual users.
- **Target Audience**:
  - Students who need an affordable and functional laptop for schoolwork.
  - Casual users who require a reliable machine for browsing, streaming, and everyday tasks.
  - Families looking for a general-purpose home laptop.

Essential Factors to Consider When Buying a Lenovo Laptop

When choosing a Lenovo laptop, several key factors should guide your decision. The right choice will depend on how you plan to use the laptop, your budget, and specific features that matter most to you.

1. Performance

Performance is often dictated by the laptop's processor (CPU), graphics card (GPU), RAM, and storage. Lenovo offers laptops equipped with the latest Intel and AMD processors, along with options for discrete graphics cards for gamers and creators.

- **For general use**: Intel Core i3/i5 or AMD Ryzen 3/5 with integrated graphics should be sufficient.
- **For professional use**: Opt for Intel Core i7/i9 or AMD Ryzen 7/9 for heavier tasks like video editing, 3D rendering, or software development.
- **For gaming**: Look for laptops with dedicated GPUs like NVIDIA's GeForce series or AMD's Radeon graphics cards.

2. Portability

Portability is crucial for those who travel frequently or need a laptop they can easily carry around. Weight, thickness, and battery life are all important considerations.

- **Ultraportable laptops** like the ThinkPad X1 Carbon or Yoga series are ideal for users who prioritise mobility. These laptops are lightweight and offer long battery life without compromising on performance.
- **Heavier laptops** like the Legion series are built for performance but may be bulkier due to more powerful components and larger screens.

3. Design and Build Quality

Lenovo offers a range of designs, from premium metal builds to more budget-friendly plastic chassis. If you need a device that can withstand wear and tear, the ThinkPad series is renowned for its durable construction, often tested against military standards for ruggedness.

- **For premium design**: Yoga and ThinkPad models often feature high-end materials such as carbon fibre and aluminium, ensuring durability and a professional look.
- **For budget-conscious buyers**: IdeaPad and ThinkBook models offer functional designs with plastic builds that still look modern and sleek but at a lower cost.

4. Display Quality

The quality of the display is important for tasks like content creation, gaming, or simply watching movies. Lenovo offers various resolutions and display types depending on the series.

- **For creatives and gamers**: Look for models with high-resolution displays (1440p or 4K) and support for a wide colour gamut, such as those in the Yoga and Legion series.

- **For general use**: A 1080p display should suffice, which is commonly found in ThinkBooks and IdeaPads.

5. Battery Life

Battery life is essential for those who need to work on the go or away from power outlets for extended periods. Laptops like the ThinkPad X1 and Yoga series are known for their excellent battery performance, often lasting over 10 hours on a single charge.

Target Users for Each Lenovo Laptop Series

Each Lenovo series is designed with specific user groups in mind:

- **Yoga**: Ideal for creatives, multitaskers, and professionals who need flexibility. The 2-in-1 design makes it suitable for both work and entertainment.
- **ThinkBook**: Tailored for young professionals, entrepreneurs, and small

business owners looking for a balance of performance and affordability.

- **Legion**: Aimed at gamers and high-performance users who require powerful hardware for gaming, video editing, and other intensive tasks.
- **ThinkPad**: The go-to option for business professionals, corporate users, and anyone needing a reliable, durable, and secure work laptop.
- **IdeaPad**: Best for students, casual users, and families looking for a budget-friendly option that can handle everyday computing tasks.

Understanding Lenovo Hardware: Inside the Machine

Lenovo laptops are known for their performance, durability, and innovative hardware configurations, making them some of the most popular choices in both consumer and business markets. While the outer design often captures attention, the internal components such as processors, RAM, GPUs, and cooling systems define the real capability of these machines. To fully understand Lenovo's approach to hardware, it's essential to examine these key elements in detail, explore Lenovo's incorporation of AI processors and the AI Core chip, and understand the significance of their thermal solutions and battery technologies.

Key Components Inside Lenovo Laptops

The internal hardware of any laptop plays a critical role in determining its performance, speed, and efficiency. In Lenovo laptops, these components are carefully selected to meet the diverse needs of users, from casual users to power-hungry professionals.

1. Processors (CPUs)

The processor, often referred to as the brain of the computer, handles most of the computational tasks and dictates the speed and multitasking capability of the laptop. Lenovo uses a range of processors, from Intel and AMD, across their laptop models.

- **Intel Processors**: Many Lenovo laptops, particularly in the ThinkPad, ThinkBook, and IdeaPad lines, are equipped with Intel's Core series of processors. Intel offers a wide range of processors from **Core i3** (for basic tasks) to **Core i9** (for high-performance tasks such as gaming, 3D rendering, and large-scale data processing). In recent years, Lenovo has also integrated Intel's **Evo platform** in certain models, ensuring better battery life, responsiveness, and advanced AI capabilities.

- **AMD Processors**: Lenovo has increasingly embraced AMD's Ryzen processors, which have gained popularity due to their exceptional multi-threaded performance and competitive pricing. Laptops featuring **AMD Ryzen 5** and **Ryzen 7** processors offer strong competition to their Intel counterparts, especially for multitasking and creative workloads like video editing.

- **Target Use**:

- ○ **Basic Tasks** (web browsing, light document editing): Intel Core i3, AMD Ryzen 3.
- ○ **Everyday Use** (multitasking, productivity, entertainment): Intel Core i5, AMD Ryzen 5.
- ○ **Heavy-Duty Use** (gaming, content creation, professional software): Intel Core i7/i9, AMD Ryzen 7/9.

2. Graphics Processing Units (GPUs)

The GPU plays a significant role in rendering graphics, especially for gaming, creative software, and handling large datasets. Lenovo offers both integrated and dedicated GPU options depending on the laptop model.

- **Integrated Graphics**: Many Lenovo laptops, particularly those geared towards general productivity, come with integrated graphics, such as **Intel Iris Xe** or **AMD Radeon** integrated solutions. While sufficient for basic tasks and even light photo editing or casual gaming, integrated graphics are not ideal for resource-intensive applications like modern AAA games or 3D modelling.

- **Dedicated Graphics**: For users requiring more graphical power, Lenovo offers models equipped with dedicated GPUs, such as **NVIDIA GeForce GTX** or **RTX** in their Legion and select ThinkPad models. NVIDIA's **RTX series** is especially known for ray tracing technology and AI-enhanced performance, making it perfect for gaming and creative professionals who need more power for tasks such as 3D rendering, video editing, and deep learning.
- **Target Use**:
  - **Basic Users**: Integrated Intel UHD or Iris Xe, AMD Radeon integrated graphics.
  - **Creative Professionals and Gamers**: NVIDIA GeForce GTX/RTX or AMD Radeon RX.

3. RAM (Random Access Memory)

RAM is crucial for multitasking and running applications smoothly. Lenovo laptops typically come with a variety of RAM configurations, allowing users to choose based on their needs.

- **Typical Configurations**: Lenovo laptops often start with **4GB or 8GB** of RAM for lower-end models and extend up to **16GB or 32GB** in high-performance models such as the Legion or ThinkPad P series. RAM is particularly important for users who work with large files, run multiple applications simultaneously, or use memory-intensive software.
- **Target Use**:
  - **Light Tasks**: 4GB – 8GB RAM.
  - **Everyday Multitasking and Productivity**: 8GB – 16GB RAM.
  - **Heavy Use and Professional Applications**: 16GB – 32GB RAM.

4. Storage (SSD vs. HDD)

Storage technology has evolved significantly, with Lenovo laptops primarily shifting towards

Solid-State Drives (SSD), which offer faster read and write speeds, making laptops more responsive and improving boot times.

- **SSD**: Most Lenovo models come with **NVMe SSDs**, which are much faster than traditional hard drives (HDD). They allow faster file transfers, quicker system startups, and more seamless application launches. Sizes range from **256GB** to **1TB** or more, depending on the laptop.
- **HDD**: Lenovo occasionally includes **HDDs** in their lower-end models or as secondary drives in some Legion or workstation models for users who need massive storage capacity at a lower price, but they're slower compared to SSDs.
- **Target Use**:
    - **Everyday Users**: 256GB – 512GB SSD.
    - **Gamers and Creatives**: 512GB – 1TB SSD.
    - **Storage-Heavy Workloads**: HDD as a secondary option.

Lenovo's Use of AI Processors and Lenovo AI Core Chip

AI (Artificial Intelligence) is increasingly becoming an essential component in modern laptops, with Lenovo leading the charge by incorporating **AI processors** and the **Lenovo AI Core chip** into several models. These technologies bring intelligent features to the device that enhance both user experience and performance.

- **Lenovo AI Core**: This is Lenovo's AI-focused chip that works to enhance system security, manage power consumption, and optimise performance dynamically. The AI Core analyses user behaviour to predict which applications need more processing power and adjusts the CPU and GPU resources accordingly. This results in better efficiency, smoother multitasking, and extended battery life. Additionally, the AI Core provides hardware-level security, protecting the system from firmware-level attacks.

- **AI-Enhanced Features**:
  - **Performance Optimization**: AI algorithms in Lenovo laptops can automatically allocate system resources to ensure optimal performance based on real-time usage.
  - **Battery Life Management**: AI helps in conserving battery by dynamically adjusting screen brightness, CPU usage, and cooling systems to extend usage time.
  - **Security**: The AI Core chip adds another layer of security, protecting sensitive data by isolating critical tasks from potential threats.

Thermal Solutions and Battery Life Technology

Efficient cooling and battery longevity are crucial for laptop performance, especially for users engaging in intensive tasks like gaming or content creation. Lenovo has invested heavily in developing effective thermal solutions and advanced battery technologies.

1. Thermal Solutions

Managing heat is critical in laptops, particularly in high-performance models like the Legion gaming series or ThinkPad workstations. Lenovo has developed a range of cooling technologies to ensure that their laptops maintain optimal temperatures under load.

- **Legion Coldfront Technology**: The Legion series, designed for gaming, uses **Coldfront 4.0**, which consists of dual-fan systems, vapour chambers, and strategically placed heat sinks. This keeps the laptop cool even during extended gaming sessions.
- **ThinkPad Cooling Systems**: Business users may not push their laptops to the same extremes as gamers, but Lenovo has developed cooling systems that ensure

ThinkPads remain cool during heavy multitasking or use of intensive software.

2. Battery Life Technology

Lenovo's battery technology is equally advanced, with many models featuring **Rapid Charge** technology that allows users to charge their laptop quickly. ThinkPad models, for example, can often recharge up to 80% in just an hour, thanks to this technology.

- **Power Management**: Lenovo laptops use AI-based power management systems that learn user habits and optimise power distribution for the best possible battery life.
- **Multiple Battery Options**: Many Lenovo laptops offer configurations with either **standard or extended battery life**, depending on user needs. For instance, some ThinkPads offer up to 15-20 hours of usage on a single charge.

Unpacking Lenovo's Software Ecosystem

When purchasing a Lenovo laptop, it's not just the hardware that defines the experience. Lenovo has built a comprehensive software ecosystem designed to enhance the functionality, performance, and usability of their laptops. This system is particularly useful for managing system health, keeping the machine updated, enhancing security, and even providing AI-powered features to optimise the user experience. Let's take an in-depth look at the software Lenovo pre-installs, the role of Lenovo Vantage, and the integration of AI-driven features.

Pre-installed Software and Services on Lenovo Laptops

Most Lenovo laptops come with a suite of pre-installed software and services that are specifically designed to provide users with added functionality. While some users may initially view these as "bloatware," the majority of these applications offer essential tools for maintaining the system, improving productivity, or delivering enhanced support.

1. Lenovo Vantage

Lenovo Vantage is the crown jewel of Lenovo's pre-installed software ecosystem. Designed as an all-in-one system management tool, it allows users to optimise their machine's performance, manage hardware components, and stay updated with security patches.

- **System Optimization**: One of Vantage's most useful features is the ability to keep drivers and BIOS updated automatically. With hardware updates handled in the background, the laptop remains optimised without much user intervention. Users can also fine-tune their laptop's performance, adjusting between performance and battery-saving modes depending on their needs.

- **Health Monitoring**: Vantage provides users with real-time system health diagnostics. It checks the status of critical components such as the CPU, RAM, battery, and storage drives, alerting users to potential problems before they turn into major issues.

- **Customization**: Vantage offers users the ability to customise various features of their laptops. For example, it allows for keyboard light adjustments, touchpad sensitivity settings, or even the management of connected devices like printers and external displays.

2. Lenovo Migration Assistant

Lenovo also includes tools to help users transition from their old laptops to their new

Lenovo device. The **Lenovo Migration Assistant** is designed to seamlessly transfer files, settings, and applications from an older machine to a new Lenovo laptop, without the need for external drives or manual processes. This software can connect two devices over a Wi-Fi network, speeding up what would otherwise be a tedious transfer process.

3. Lenovo Smart Performance

Some Lenovo laptops come with **Smart Performance Services**, which help maintain system health by automatically detecting and fixing system issues. This tool can remove unnecessary files, enhance system boot times, and resolve minor performance problems. Smart Performance focuses on keeping your machine running smoothly, addressing common slowdowns or bugs that may arise over time.

4. Lenovo Commercial Vantage

For business users, Lenovo pre-installs **Commercial Vantage** on many of its ThinkPad and ThinkBook models. This software helps manage business-specific features like enterprise-grade security options, hardware encryption settings, and remote management functions. IT administrators can also use this tool to configure systems for an entire office or department remotely.

Lenovo Vantage: Comprehensive System Management

Lenovo Vantage deserves further exploration due to its wide range of features designed to enhance the Lenovo laptop experience. As mentioned earlier, this software is central to many of Lenovo's devices, giving users a single location to manage everything related to their laptop's hardware, security, and performance.

1. Driver and Firmware Updates

Keeping your laptop's drivers and firmware updated is critical for optimal performance, security, and compatibility with peripherals or new software. Lenovo Vantage automates this process, notifying users when updates are available or even applying them in the background. This ensures that the system remains secure and compatible with the latest technologies, while eliminating the need for manual intervention.

2. Power and Performance Management

Lenovo Vantage includes detailed power management settings that allow users to switch between different performance modes depending on their current needs. For example, **Battery Saver Mode** can be enabled during travel to maximise battery life, while **Performance Mode** can be activated when running demanding applications like gaming or video editing software. These customizable settings provide users with control over how much power their laptop consumes.

3. Security Center

Another key component of Lenovo Vantage is the **Security Center**, which includes features like **Wi-Fi Security**, **Lenovo Enhanced Privacy Guard**, and **Camera Privacy Mode**. These tools help protect users from common cybersecurity threats by adding extra layers of security, like automatically disabling untrusted Wi-Fi connections or ensuring the camera isn't activated without consent.

4. Audio and Display Customization

Users can also manage their display settings and audio profiles directly through Vantage. For example, it supports colour calibration for users working in creative fields, allowing them to adjust colour profiles for different lighting environments. Audio settings can be tailored for different tasks, whether users are listening to music, conducting video conferences, or watching movies.

AI-Driven Features in Lenovo Laptops

One of the more recent additions to Lenovo's software ecosystem is the integration of

AI-driven features, particularly in the form of the **Lenovo AI Core chip**. These features use machine learning algorithms to improve performance, optimise energy consumption, and enhance user experience.

1. AI Performance Optimization

The AI Core chip analyses real-time user behaviour to predict which applications or tasks need more computational power and dynamically adjusts the system resources accordingly. For example, if a user is running a graphics-intensive program, the AI Core will allocate more resources to the GPU and CPU, ensuring the smooth running of the application without the need for manual adjustments.

2. AI-Powered Battery Management

Battery life is a critical concern for mobile users, and Lenovo's AI-driven software enhances battery efficiency by learning usage patterns. For instance, if the laptop detects that a user typically engages in long periods of light usage, it will reduce power consumption by dimming the screen and managing system resources more efficiently. Similarly, the AI learns when the user is likely to require higher performance and prepares the system to deliver it.

3. Intelligent Cooling System

Overheating can cause a range of issues, from reduced performance to hardware damage. Lenovo laptops equipped with AI-driven cooling systems intelligently regulate fan speeds and thermal profiles based on real-time temperature readings and workload demands. This results in quieter operation when performing light tasks and more aggressive cooling when the system is under heavy load.

4. Smart Facial Recognition and AI Security

Lenovo has integrated AI-driven **facial recognition** technology into some of its laptop models, allowing for quick and secure logins. This feature is particularly useful in environments where speed and security are priorities. Additionally, some models utilise AI-based security enhancements, such as automatic locking when the user steps away from the laptop and real-time monitoring for unusual behaviours that might indicate malware.

Yoga Series: Flexibility Meets Performance

The Lenovo Yoga series has become a staple for users seeking versatility, power, and cutting-edge technology in a single device. These laptops are known for their 2-in-1 functionality, where a laptop transforms into a tablet, offering flexibility in use cases. The Yoga series has successfully integrated features such as touch screens, stylus support, and artificial intelligence to cater to professionals who value creative freedom and productivity. One of the standout models, the **Yoga Pro 9i**, epitomises this fusion of flexibility and performance, making it an ideal choice for a wide range of users, from designers and content creators to students and multitaskers.

Lenovo Yoga Models: A Closer Look

1. Yoga Pro 9i

The **Yoga Pro 9i** is arguably one of Lenovo's most impressive models within the Yoga line, representing a blend of high-end performance with a sleek and convertible design. Built for those who demand power, this model comes with top-tier specifications such as Intel's latest processors (up to i9), NVIDIA GeForce RTX graphics, and advanced display options that are ideal for creative professionals.

- **Display Quality**: The Pro 9i offers up to a 4K OLED display, which ensures vivid colours and deep blacks, perfect for digital artists, photographers, and video editors who need precise colour accuracy. The high refresh rate also benefits those who engage in graphic-intensive work or even gaming.

- **Power Under the Hood**: With configurations that allow up to 32GB of RAM and high-speed PCIe SSD storage, the Yoga Pro 9i is built to handle intense workloads without breaking a sweat. The inclusion of NVIDIA RTX graphics makes it possible for users to render 3D models, work with large datasets, or edit 4K videos efficiently.

- **2-in-1 Functionality**: What sets this laptop apart from traditional clamshell designs is its convertible nature. The Yoga Pro 9i can switch seamlessly between laptop mode for standard work, tent mode for presentations, stand mode for media consumption, and tablet mode for drawing or note-taking using the Lenovo Precision Pen.

2. Yoga 7i

The **Yoga 7i** targets a broader audience, offering premium features at a more accessible price point. While it doesn't match the raw power of the Yoga Pro 9i, it is still well-suited for users who require a high degree of versatility without needing workstation-grade components.

- **Performance**: The Yoga 7i is powered by Intel Core i5 or i7 processors, with integrated Intel Iris Xe graphics. This configuration is ideal for daily productivity tasks, light content creation, and multitasking. It's an excellent choice for students or professionals who want a machine that can handle presentations, light photo editing, and video conferencing.
- **Portability**: One of the highlights of the Yoga 7i is its portability. Weighing around 3.2 pounds and featuring a thin profile, it's highly portable without sacrificing performance. The all-day battery life, which can last up to 13 hours on a single charge, adds another layer of convenience for those constantly on the go.

3. Yoga Slim 7i Carbon

For those who prioritise portability above all else, the **Yoga Slim 7i Carbon** offers a feather-light, ultra-thin design without compromising on performance. Designed with professionals and frequent travellers in mind, the Slim 7i Carbon weighs less than 1 kg, making it one of the lightest laptops in the market.

- **Durability**: Despite its lightweight frame, the laptop's carbon-fibre construction ensures durability, resisting wear and tear that often accompanies frequent travel.
- **Battery Life and Power Efficiency**: It offers exceptional battery life, thanks to Intel's low-power processors and Lenovo's intelligent power-saving features. The machine's adaptive performance, which adjusts to user needs, helps conserve power during light tasks and optimises it for heavier applications like photo editing.

Key Features of the Yoga Series

The Yoga series is not just about performance on paper but about how its design and features cater to different types of users. The combination of functionality, aesthetics, and technology makes these laptops stand out from the competition.

1. 2-in-1 Functionality

A core feature of the Yoga line is its **360-degree hinge**, allowing for multiple modes of use. This flexibility provides users with a variety of ways to interact with the device based on their specific needs.

- **Laptop Mode**: Ideal for typing, browsing, and productivity work.
- **Tent Mode**: Convenient for presentations or video watching, especially in small spaces.
- **Stand Mode**: Perfect for media consumption or interactive applications.
- **Tablet Mode**: With a responsive touchscreen and stylus support, this mode shines for artists, designers, and note-takers.

2. Touch Screens and Pen Integration

Most Yoga models feature **touchscreen displays** and are compatible with the **Lenovo Precision Pen**, making them an ideal tool for creatives. Whether sketching, annotating documents, or taking notes, the stylus adds a new level of interaction with the device. The responsiveness and accuracy of the touch input make these laptops stand out for users in design-related fields.

3. AI Integration

Lenovo has made a substantial investment in artificial intelligence integration across its devices, and the Yoga series is no exception.

- **AI-Powered Performance**: Laptops like the Yoga Pro 9i come with Lenovo's **AI Core** technology, which adjusts power and performance based on user habits. This means that the laptop intelligently allocates resources to the tasks you're

working on, helping to prolong battery life
and reduce unnecessary heat generation.

- **AI Noise Cancellation**: For remote
workers or frequent video call users,
AI-driven noise cancellation features help
filter out background noise, providing
clearer audio during calls.

Who Should Use the Lenovo Yoga Series?

The versatility of the Yoga series makes it
suitable for a wide range of users, but there are
specific groups that can maximise its benefits:

1. Creative Professionals

The Yoga series, particularly models like the
Yoga Pro 9i, are built for **graphic designers**,
photographers, **video editors**, and **illustrators**.
The high-resolution, colour-accurate screens,
combined with the stylus support and powerful
internal components, offer a portable
workstation that caters to their demanding
workflows.

2. Multitaskers and Office Workers

For those who juggle multiple tasks at once, the Yoga series provides the flexibility and power needed to keep up with busy schedules. The ability to switch between modes means users can adapt the device to whatever task is at hand, whether that's typing out reports, conducting video calls, or presenting to clients.

3. Students

For students who require a machine for taking notes, completing assignments, and watching lectures, the Yoga series offers the perfect combination of portability, battery life, and functionality. Models like the Yoga 7i provide excellent all-around performance at a more affordable price point.

ThinkPad and ThinkBook Series: Built for Business

The **ThinkPad** and **ThinkBook** series by Lenovo have long been synonymous with business productivity, reliability, and durability. While the ThinkPad has become a mainstay in corporate environments and has a legacy stretching back decades, the ThinkBook line is a more recent addition aimed at small and medium businesses, offering a balance between modern design and professional performance. Both lines are built with enterprise users in mind, focusing on security, durability, and the applications necessary to thrive in the business world.

Evolution of the ThinkPad Line: A Legacy of Business Excellence

The **ThinkPad** series traces its origins to IBM, with the first ThinkPad released in **1992**. Since then, it has evolved into one of the most trusted brands in the business laptop market. Known for its durability, reliability, and minimalist design, the ThinkPad quickly became the go-to choice for professionals who required a machine capable of handling demanding tasks in corporate environments.

The iconic **TrackPoint** (the red dot in the centre of the keyboard), rugged build quality, and spill-resistant keyboards became hallmarks of the ThinkPad brand. Even after Lenovo acquired IBM's personal computing division in 2005, the ThinkPad's legacy continued. Lenovo kept the same attention to quality and innovation while improving hardware specifications, making the ThinkPad one of the most recognizable business laptops globally.

- **ThinkPad X1 Carbon**: A pivotal model in the ThinkPad evolution, the **X1 Carbon** introduced ultra-lightweight carbon fibre construction with advanced features such as extended battery life, security enhancements, and high-end performance. This model, especially in its newer generations, is one of the most recommended ultrabooks for business users due to its portability without sacrificing power.

Introduction to the ThinkBook Line: A Modern Business Approach

While the ThinkPad is geared toward more traditional corporate users, Lenovo introduced the **ThinkBook** series in 2019 to target a younger, modern workforce, including small and medium businesses (SMBs) and entrepreneurial users. ThinkBooks were designed to offer a mix of professional-grade performance with consumer-friendly design elements, like slim form factors and brushed-metal finishes.

ThinkBooks are positioned as slightly less robust than ThinkPads but still offer business-class features such as **enterprise-grade security**, **enhanced collaboration tools**, and **power-efficient processors**. With these models, Lenovo aimed to cater to businesses that need more affordable options without compromising essential business functionalities.

Focus on Security, Durability, and Business Applications

Both the ThinkPad and ThinkBook series emphasise features that enhance security, durability, and productivity, making them ideal for business use.

1. Security Features

- **ThinkPad Security**: ThinkPads are known for their top-tier security features. They often come equipped with **TPM (Trusted Platform Module)** chips for hardware-level encryption, **biometric authentication** like fingerprint readers, and optional **IR cameras** for facial recognition via Windows Hello. Additionally, ThinkPad models often have **privacy shutters** for the webcam and options for **self-healing BIOS**, ensuring data integrity even after firmware issues.

- **ThinkBook Security**: The ThinkBook series, while generally more affordable than the ThinkPad line, still maintains robust security. ThinkBooks also feature **TPM 2.0 chips, fingerprint readers integrated into the power button**, and webcam privacy shutters. These features allow small businesses to benefit from the same level of data protection found in more premium corporate laptops.

2. Durability

- **ThinkPad Durability**: ThinkPads have a reputation for being nearly indestructible. These laptops undergo **MIL-STD-810G military-grade testing**, ensuring that they can withstand harsh environments, temperature fluctuations, and accidental drops. Their spill-resistant keyboards and durable chassis make them a favourite for professionals who need a reliable machine on the go.

- **ThinkBook Durability**: Although ThinkBooks are more stylish and lighter, they still boast a respectable level of durability. Most ThinkBooks are **aluminium or metal-clad**, providing a premium feel and decent protection against everyday wear and tear. They also undergo a series of durability tests to ensure reliability.

3. Business Applications

- **ThinkPad Business Tools**: ThinkPads often come preloaded with business-oriented software such as **Lenovo Vantage**, a powerful tool that helps users manage system updates, security features, and power settings. Additionally, many models come equipped with **Thunderbolt 4** ports, allowing fast data transfers and support for multiple external displays—essential for professionals in data-heavy fields.

- **ThinkBook Business Tools**: ThinkBooks are also geared toward productivity, featuring software like **Lenovo Commercial Vantage**, which gives users control over system settings. The models typically feature **USB-C** ports for fast charging and data transfers, and some models even come with **dual SSD options** for added storage flexibility.

Reviews of ThinkBook 13x Gen 4 and Other Notable Models

ThinkBook 13x Gen 4

The **ThinkBook 13x Gen 4** is a standout in the ThinkBook series, offering a slim, modern design with enough power to cater to business users who value both aesthetics and performance.

- **Display**: The 13x Gen 4 features a 13.3-inch **WQXGA (2560 x 1600)** display, providing crisp visuals and excellent colour accuracy. This makes it suitable not only for office tasks but also for light creative work such as graphic design.

- **Performance**: Powered by Intel's **12th Gen Core processors**, the ThinkBook 13x can handle demanding workloads, including multitasking with large Excel sheets, browsing, and video calls. With **16GB of RAM** and fast **SSD storage**, this model can easily handle the day-to-day demands of business professionals.
- **Design and Portability**: One of the key advantages of the ThinkBook 13x Gen 4 is its slim profile, measuring just **12.9mm thick** and weighing **under 1.2 kg**. This makes it highly portable without compromising on build quality. It has a sleek aluminium finish, adding to its premium appeal.
- **AI-Powered Features**: This model incorporates AI-driven enhancements, such as **noise-cancelling microphones**

and **smart power management**, making it ideal for professionals who frequently attend virtual meetings or work in noisy environments.

ThinkPad X1 Carbon Gen 9

The **ThinkPad X1 Carbon Gen 9** continues to be a flagship in Lenovo's business lineup. Known for its **ultralight carbon fibre body**, it offers best-in-class features like **5G connectivity**, **4K display options**, and **Intel Evo** certification, ensuring fast performance and extended battery life.

- **Business Use**: The X1 Carbon is perfect for C-suite executives, consultants, or those who need a highly portable yet powerful machine. With a battery life of **up to 15 hours**, it's tailored for professionals who need a reliable machine while travelling.

ThinkBook 16p Gen 3

For those looking for a larger screen in a business laptop, the **ThinkBook 16p Gen 3** is an excellent option. It combines **AMD Ryzen 9 processors** with **NVIDIA RTX 3060** graphics, making it suitable for both business tasks and more demanding creative applications.

- **Performance**: This model stands out for its ability to handle heavy multitasking, video editing, and 3D rendering while maintaining business-friendly features such as **fingerprint security** and **enterprise-grade performance**.

Legion Series: Gaming and Performance Unleashed

The **Lenovo Legion series** represents Lenovo's premier line of gaming laptops, offering high-performance hardware tailored to gamers, content creators, and power users. Built to handle resource-intensive games and applications, these laptops are known for their balance of cutting-edge technology, robust cooling systems, and design features that cater to the needs of both professional gamers and creative professionals.

Overview of the Legion Series: A Perfect Fusion of Power and Design

Lenovo's **Legion series** was developed to meet the rising demand for powerful gaming laptops without compromising portability or design. Unlike traditional gaming laptops, which often have bulky and flashy designs, Lenovo has opted for a more subdued aesthetic with sleek, minimalist exteriors combined with high-performance internals.

The Legion series is built with gamers and creators in mind, meaning that these laptops aren't just suited for AAA gaming titles but are also capable of handling resource-heavy tasks like 3D rendering, video editing, and digital art creation. The powerful combination of high-refresh-rate displays, NVIDIA's advanced GPUs, Intel's and AMD's latest processors, and Lenovo's proprietary cooling technology makes the Legion series a reliable choice for those requiring peak performance.

Thermal Solutions: The Legion Coldfront Hyper Thermal Technology

One of the most critical aspects of any gaming laptop is how it manages heat. High-performance components like **NVIDIA GPUs** and **Intel Core or AMD Ryzen processors** generate significant amounts of heat during intense workloads. The **Legion Coldfront Thermal Technology** is Lenovo's solution to this challenge.

Coldfront Features

The **Legion Coldfront Hyper Thermal** system includes several features that allow these laptops to run cooler and more efficiently, even during extended gaming sessions or under heavy workloads.

- **Advanced Quad-Channel Cooling**: The Legion series typically features a **quad-channel ventilation system**. This allows more efficient airflow, ensuring that both the CPU and GPU are kept at optimal temperatures during high-stress tasks. This system channels cool air through multiple points and expels hot air through rear and side vents, reducing the likelihood of thermal throttling, which can impact performance.

- **Liquid Crystal Polymer Fans**: Lenovo has integrated **liquid crystal polymer blades** in the fans of its Legion laptops, making the fans thinner but more durable. This ensures greater airflow while keeping fan noise to a minimum. These improvements also contribute to the longevity of the cooling system.

- **Thermal Sensors**: With **thermally tuned sensors**, the system automatically adjusts fan speeds based on real-time temperature readings, ensuring that the components remain within safe operating limits without sacrificing performance.

- **Vapour Chamber Technology**: The **Legion 7i** and higher-end models often include vapour chamber technology that maximises heat dissipation by spreading heat across a larger surface area, allowing for more efficient cooling compared to traditional heat pipes.

NVIDIA Graphics and Cutting-Edge Displays: Immersive Gaming Experience

Graphics performance is critical for gaming, and Lenovo doesn't disappoint in this regard. The Legion series is equipped with some of the latest **NVIDIA GeForce RTX** GPUs, which are not only capable of running the latest AAA games at high frame rates but also support advanced features like **ray tracing** and **AI-enhanced** rendering techniques.

Key GPU Features

- **Ray Tracing**: NVIDIA's **RTX series** GPUs, found in models like the **Legion 7i**, enable real-time ray tracing, which simulates the way light interacts with objects in a game environment. This leads to more realistic shadows, reflections, and lighting effects, providing a more immersive gaming experience.

- **DLSS (Deep Learning Super Sampling)**: With NVIDIA's **DLSS** technology, supported in Legion models, gamers can enjoy higher resolutions without compromising frame rates. This AI-driven feature boosts performance by rendering images at a lower resolution and then using machine learning to upscale them, maintaining image quality.

- **High Refresh Rate Displays**: The Legion series also stands out with its displays, many of which offer **120Hz, 144Hz, and even 165Hz** refresh rates, combined with **FHD** (1920x1080) or **QHD** (2560x1440) resolutions. These high-refresh-rate screens reduce motion blur and enhance responsiveness, giving gamers a competitive edge in fast-paced titles like first-person shooters and racing games.

Comparing Legion Models: Legion 7i and Other Variants

Lenovo's Legion lineup offers several different models, each catering to slightly different segments of the gaming and content creation market. Here's a closer look at a few standout models.

1. Legion 7i: Flagship Gaming Powerhouse

The **Legion 7i** is Lenovo's top-of-the-line model and is designed for hardcore gamers and creators who need the highest possible performance. Key features of this model include:

- **NVIDIA RTX 3080/3070 GPUs**: These powerful graphics cards allow the 7i to run the latest games on ultra settings and deliver stunning visual effects for creative applications.
- **11th or 12th Gen Intel Core i7/i9 Processors**: The Legion 7i is powered by the latest high-performance Intel processors, which handle multitasking and

77

CPU-heavy applications like rendering or video editing with ease.

- **Up to 32GB DDR4 RAM**: With up to **32GB of RAM**, this model can handle numerous applications and tasks simultaneously without any slowdown, perfect for gaming, streaming, and professional work.
- **QHD Display with 165Hz**: The Legion 7i often comes equipped with a **16-inch QHD display**, providing crisp image quality and a smooth refresh rate for a premium gaming experience.
- **AI Optimised Performance**: Lenovo's AI-enhanced technology dynamically adjusts system performance based on the workload, ensuring that users get the most out of their hardware without overheating or throttling.

2. Legion 5i: Mainstream Gaming Performance

The **Legion 5i** series offers a more budget-friendly option for gamers without sacrificing too much in terms of performance. It comes with **RTX 3060** or **RTX 3050** GPUs, making it capable of running AAA games at medium to high settings.

- **Balanced Cooling**: While it doesn't have the vapour chamber tech of the Legion 7i, the **Coldfront 3.0** cooling system still keeps temperatures under control during intense gaming.
- **Solid Build Quality**: The **Legion 5i** maintains a high-quality design with a durable aluminium chassis, offering a professional look that suits both gamers and professionals.
- **Affordable Display Options**: The Legion 5i typically includes a **1080p display** with options for **144Hz refresh rates**, providing a smooth gaming experience without breaking the bank.

3. Legion Slim 7i: Portability Meets Performance

For those who prioritise portability but still want a capable gaming machine, the **Legion Slim 7i** is a fantastic choice.

- **NVIDIA RTX 2060 Max-Q**: The **Max-Q** variant of the **RTX 2060** offers a great balance between power and efficiency, allowing for gaming on the go without compromising battery life or creating excess heat.
- **Thin and Light Design**: As the name suggests, the **Slim 7i** is designed to be highly portable, with a thin profile and lightweight build that makes it easier to carry around compared to other gaming laptops.
- **Battery Efficiency**: The Slim 7i comes with **improved battery life** compared to traditional gaming laptops, and its power-efficient display options further extend usage between charges.

Ideal Use Cases for Gamers and Creators

The **Lenovo Legion series** doesn't just cater to gamers. Thanks to its powerful hardware and feature set, these laptops are also excellent for **content creators**, **designers**, and **video editors** who need high performance for rendering, multitasking, and working with large files.

1. Gamers

- **Competitive Gamers**: With high-refresh-rate displays and powerful GPUs, Legion laptops are ideal for competitive players of **first-person shooters** and **battle royale** games where quick reflexes and low latency are essential.
- **Casual Gamers**: Even the lower-end Legion models provide a smooth experience for casual gamers who enjoy single-player titles or less graphically intensive games.

2. Creative Professionals

- **3D Modelers and Animators**: The **ray-tracing capabilities** of NVIDIA RTX GPUs make the Legion series a powerful tool for **3D modelling** and **animation** software, allowing artists to preview scenes in real time with accurate lighting and shadows.

- **Video Editors**: The Legion's fast CPUs, large memory options, and **fast SSDs** are perfect for handling large video files and running video editing software like **Adobe Premiere Pro** or **DaVinci Resolve**.

Maximising Your Lenovo Laptop: Tips, Tricks, and Hacks

Lenovo laptops, whether they are from the ThinkPad, Legion, Yoga, or IdeaPad series, are known for their versatility and reliable performance. However, like any piece of technology, to truly get the most out of your device, a few optimizations and careful management can go a long way. In this chapter, we'll cover practical tips and hacks that will help you maximise your Lenovo laptop's potential, extending battery life, improving performance, and ensuring the machine stays efficient over time.

Battery Management: How to Make Your Lenovo Laptop Last Longer

Battery life is a concern for every laptop user, especially those who need their device to run for extended periods without access to power outlets. Lenovo offers built-in tools and settings that help optimise battery usage, but with a few additional tricks, you can get even more juice out of your device.

Lenovo Vantage Battery Conservation Mode

Lenovo laptops come with **Lenovo Vantage** software, which is a powerful tool to help manage various aspects of your device, including battery settings. One particularly useful feature is the **Battery Conservation Mode**, which keeps the battery charged at around 55-60% when plugged in. This extends the lifespan of your battery, especially if you use your laptop mostly while connected to power.

Power Plans and Display Settings

Utilising **Windows Power Plans** is another important way to manage your battery life. For day-to-day tasks like web browsing and document editing, the **Power Saver Plan** is ideal. If you need more performance for intensive tasks, you can switch to the **High-Performance Plan** but remember this will consume more energy.

Additionally, reducing your **screen brightness** and enabling **Night Light Mode** can greatly help conserve power. Lenovo laptops, particularly ThinkPads and Legion models, have power-efficient display technologies that adjust brightness based on ambient light. Make sure to enable these adaptive brightness features.

Managing Background Applications

Applications running in the background can drain battery life and consume unnecessary resources. Use the **Task Manager** (Ctrl+Shift+Esc) to monitor and close apps or services you don't need. On Lenovo machines, **Vantage Smart Performance Services** can help by automatically identifying resource-heavy applications and offering suggestions on how to manage them.

Enhancing Performance: Getting the Best Out of Your Lenovo Laptop

If you're looking for better speed, smoother multitasking, or even improved gaming performance, there are several ways you can optimise your Lenovo laptop to deliver peak performance.

1. Keep Your System Updated

Regular updates ensure that your laptop is running on the latest drivers and security patches. Use **Lenovo Vantage** to manage system updates, especially for BIOS and chipset drivers, which can directly impact performance.

2. Optimise Startup Programs

By default, many applications are set to launch at startup, which can significantly slow down boot times and affect system speed. To control this, go to the **Task Manager** and navigate to the **Startup** tab. Disable any unnecessary programs from launching at boot.

3. Use SSD Optimization Tools

Most Lenovo laptops come with fast **Solid State Drives (SSDs)**. However, to maintain optimal SSD performance, use tools such as **Windows' Disk Cleanup** and **Lenovo's Vantage Storage Health** features to ensure your drives remain clean and efficient. Avoid filling your SSD beyond 70% of its total capacity to keep performance at its peak.

4. Enable Performance Mode for Intensive Tasks

In Lenovo laptops, especially in the Legion and ThinkPad series, you can switch between power profiles using **Lenovo Vantage**. For tasks like gaming or 3D rendering, enable **Performance**

Mode, which allocates more resources and power to your GPU and CPU, ensuring you get the best out of your laptop.

Optimising System Settings for Productivity and Longevity

The longevity and efficiency of your Lenovo laptop don't just depend on hardware. Optimising system settings can play a huge role in keeping your machine running smoothly for years.

Regular Cleanup and Disk Management

Ensure that you perform regular cleanups of temporary files and unnecessary applications. The **Storage Sense** feature in Windows can automatically delete old or unused files to free up space. Additionally, Lenovo Vantage offers **PC Health Check** and **Smart Performance Services**, which scan your system for issues and provide actionable steps to fix them.

Keep Your Laptop Cool

Overheating is a common problem with high-performance laptops. Use cooling pads and make sure that your laptop's vents are not obstructed when using it on soft surfaces like beds or couches. **Legion Coldfront** thermal management features in Lenovo's Legion laptops help regulate temperature, but additional cooling can prevent long-term heat damage.

Regular Dusting and Cleaning

Physically cleaning your Lenovo laptop can also enhance performance. Dust accumulating around vents and fans can cause overheating and reduce airflow. Use a can of compressed air to clean the vents every few months. This simple maintenance can prevent thermal throttling, where the CPU or GPU slows down to avoid overheating.

Disabling Unnecessary Visual Effects

While Windows 10 and 11 come with great visual effects, they can tax your system's performance. To disable these, go to **System**

Properties > **Performance Options**, and select **Adjust for best performance**. You can manually pick which visual effects you want to keep or turn off for a balance between aesthetics and performance.

Keeping Your Lenovo Running Efficiently Over Time

Laptops, like any other piece of technology, tend to slow down over time. By following the right maintenance practices, you can ensure that your Lenovo device continues to perform well for years to come.

Regular Backup and Cleanup

Over time, laptops accumulate unnecessary files, software, and data. Regularly backup your important files using **OneDrive** or **external storage**, then clean out old data. This ensures that your system remains uncluttered, which improves both boot speed and overall performance.

Monitor System Temperatures

Use Lenovo Vantage to keep track of system temperatures, particularly during gaming or other intensive tasks. Prolonged overheating can degrade your CPU and GPU performance over time. If you notice temperature spikes, clean the vents and consider investing in a cooling pad.

Battery Care

If you use your laptop on AC power frequently, enable **Battery Conservation Mode** to avoid overcharging the battery. Also, avoid deep discharges where the battery level falls below 20%, as this can reduce battery lifespan. Perform full charge cycles occasionally to recalibrate the battery's charging capacity.

Run Security and Malware Scans

Regular malware scans using **Windows Defender** or third-party antivirus software can keep your system free of harmful programs that may slow down your machine. Lenovo's **ThinkShield** platform also provides enhanced security for ThinkPad users, including a secure BIOS and advanced encryption features to protect sensitive data.

Additional Tips and Useful Lenovo Shortcuts

- **Keyboard Shortcuts**: Lenovo keyboards often come with unique keys such as the **Fn+Q** combination to toggle between performance modes (quiet, balanced, and performance). Use **Fn+Space** to adjust the keyboard backlight, and **Fn+Esc** to lock the Function key in "Always On" mode for quicker access.

- **Lenovo Display Optimizations**: In the **Yoga** and **IdeaPad** series, Lenovo offers built-in tools for colour calibration, especially useful for content creators and professionals who work with photos and video editing. Make sure you adjust your display to match your workflow requirements.

- **Regular Restarts**: A simple but effective way to maintain performance is to restart your Lenovo laptop periodically. Restarting clears system memory, closes background processes, and applies critical updates that may be pending.

Lenovo Support and Services: Navigating Customer Care

Lenovo, one of the world's leading PC manufacturers, places a high emphasis on customer support, offering a wide range of services to assist users with their devices. Whether you're troubleshooting common issues, seeking warranty information, or looking for extended service options, Lenovo has created an extensive support infrastructure to help its customers.

Accessing Lenovo Customer Support

Lenovo's customer support system is designed to provide quick and efficient solutions for a variety of concerns. There are several ways to access support:

- **Lenovo Support Website**: The primary portal for customer support is the official Lenovo Support website. Here, users can find resources for their specific device, including driver downloads, user guides, and software updates. This portal also allows you to submit service requests and track the status of ongoing repairs.
- **Lenovo Vantage Software**: Most Lenovo laptops come pre-installed with Lenovo Vantage, a powerful tool that provides real-time system updates, battery optimization, and direct access to customer support. Vantage also allows users to perform system diagnostics,

monitor device health, and troubleshoot common issues independently.

- **Phone and Chat Support**: For more complex issues, Lenovo offers phone and live chat support. These services provide users with immediate assistance from technical professionals, ensuring prompt responses to critical concerns like device malfunctions or warranty claims.

Warranty Options: Protecting Your Investment

Lenovo provides comprehensive warranty services for all its products, ensuring that users are covered in the event of hardware defects or failures. Understanding the various warranty options can help users make informed decisions about the best coverage for their devices.

Standard Warranty

All Lenovo products come with a **standard warranty**, typically lasting **12 to 24 months**. This warranty covers hardware defects and provides access to repair or replacement services for faulty components. Lenovo's standard warranty also includes mail-in or carry-in services depending on the region.

Extended Warranty Options

For those who want longer protection, Lenovo offers **extended warranty plans**, which prolong the standard warranty period. These extensions can be particularly useful for users who plan to use their devices for multiple years or rely heavily on their laptops for professional work.

Extended warranties can be purchased at the time of the device purchase or added before the standard warranty expires. It's a flexible option for users who want additional peace of mind.

Repair Services: Ensuring Smooth Device Functionality

Lenovo provides several repair service options depending on the nature of the problem and the warranty status of the device. These services aim to provide users with the most efficient and convenient repair experience possible.

On-Site Repair

For business and professional users, Lenovo offers **on-site repair services**, meaning a technician can visit the customer's location to fix the issue. This is particularly useful for professionals who rely on their devices and cannot afford extended downtime.

Mail-In Repair

In cases where the device needs extensive repairs, Lenovo offers **mail-in services**. Users can ship their laptops to an authorised Lenovo repair centre, where technicians will diagnose and fix the problem before shipping the device back. This process can take a few days, depending on the severity of the issue and the availability of replacement parts.

Self-Repair Options

Lenovo also provides **self-repair options**, allowing tech-savvy users to order specific parts and fix their devices at home. This is supported by detailed repair guides and manuals available through Lenovo's official website.

Troubleshooting Common Issues: Tools and Tips

Many common issues with Lenovo laptops can be easily resolved through troubleshooting. Lenovo offers several resources to help users identify and solve problems before escalating to more comprehensive repair services.

Lenovo Vantage Diagnostics

The **Lenovo Vantage** app comes with built-in diagnostic tools that can detect and fix common issues like battery drain, performance lags, and hardware problems. Users can run these tests to get detailed reports on the health of their device and take immediate action to resolve minor issues.

Lenovo's Support Forums

For more specific issues, Lenovo's online **community forums** are a great place to seek advice. With a large user base and participation from Lenovo's own technical staff, these forums offer solutions for both common and rare issues across various devices. Users can search for their specific problem or post a new query for help from the community.

Accidental Damage Protection: Extra Peace of Mind

Beyond standard warranties, Lenovo offers **Accidental Damage Protection (ADP)**, which provides coverage for unforeseen incidents such as drops, spills, or electrical surges. Unlike the standard warranty, which covers manufacturing defects, ADP is designed to handle everyday accidents that could damage your device.

This service includes:

- **Coverage for Physical Damage**: Including drops, bumps, and cracked screens.
- **Liquid Damage**: Protection from spills or accidental submersion in liquids.
- **Electrical Surge Coverage**: Damage caused by power surges.
- **Repair or Replacement**: Depending on the extent of the damage, Lenovo will either repair or replace the affected device components.

ADP is a great option for users who work in high-risk environments or for those who want extra assurance that their investment is protected from the unpredictable.

Lenovo Premium Care: Dedicated Assistance

For users who need priority support and enhanced services, Lenovo offers **Premium Care**. This support service provides:

- **24/7 Support**: Users can contact Lenovo's technical team anytime for assistance with both hardware and software issues.
- **Faster Repair Times**: Premium Care customers are given priority when it comes to repair services, ensuring quicker turnaround times.
- **Annual PC Health Check**: Lenovo's technicians perform yearly comprehensive checkups on Premium Care devices to ensure they are running optimally.

Premium Care is ideal for professionals who need consistent support and can't afford long wait times for repairs or troubleshooting.

Extended Service Options: Covering Every Possibility

Lenovo also offers a variety of extended service options for users who need additional protection. These options provide extra coverage and faster resolution times for specific scenarios.

Smart Performance Services

Lenovo's **Smart Performance Services** offer proactive monitoring and performance enhancements for your device. This service can:

- **Identify malware threats**.
- **Optimise system speed** and remove bloatware.
- **Fix network issues**.
- **Keep your system running smoothly** through regular tune-ups.

Keep Your Drive

Lenovo's **Keep Your Drive** service allows customers to retain their storage drive in the event of a replacement, ensuring that sensitive data never leaves their possession. This is especially useful for users dealing with confidential information.

Future of Lenovo Laptops: Innovations on the Horizon

Lenovo has long been a leader in the laptop market, renowned for its robust performance, innovative designs, and commitment to user-centric technology. As the tech landscape evolves, Lenovo continues to pave the way for the future of laptops, integrating advanced technologies and responding to emerging user needs.

Integrating AI and Machine Learning

Artificial intelligence and machine learning are at the forefront of technological advancement, and Lenovo is poised to leverage these technologies to enhance user experience.

- **Smart Assistants**: Future Lenovo laptops are expected to incorporate smarter AI-driven assistants that go beyond basic functionalities. These assistants will likely anticipate user needs, offering suggestions based on habits and preferences. Imagine a device that learns when you typically start your workday, adjusting settings and pre-loading applications to streamline your workflow.

- **Performance Optimization**: AI algorithms will facilitate real-time performance tuning by analysing usage patterns and system demands. This will enable laptops to dynamically allocate resources for demanding tasks, optimising battery life, and reducing heat generation. For instance, a laptop could automatically switch to a power-saving mode during light tasks and ramp up performance during high-intensity applications such as gaming or video editing.

- **Enhanced Security Features**: Machine learning will also play a critical role in bolstering security measures. Future Lenovo laptops may implement adaptive security protocols that learn from user behaviour, identifying anomalies that could indicate security breaches. Such systems could integrate biometric authentication methods, enhancing data protection while ensuring seamless access for legitimate users.

New Form Factors and Design Innovations

As user needs evolve, so do the designs and form factors of laptops. Lenovo has a history of innovation in this area, and the future looks promising.

- **Foldable and Flexible Displays**: Building on the success of existing models, such as the Lenovo ThinkPad X1 Fold, the company is likely to expand its range of foldable laptops. These devices offer the ability to transform from a laptop to a tablet, providing unmatched versatility for professionals and creatives. Future iterations may feature enhanced durability and better hinge mechanisms, allowing for seamless transitions and more robust usage scenarios.

- **Ultra-Light and Ultra-Slim Designs**: With the rise of remote work and the need for portability, Lenovo is expected to introduce ultra-light models without compromising performance. Advances in materials science, including the use of carbon fibre and magnesium alloys, will enable the production of laptops that are not only lightweight but also durable.

- **Improved Ergonomics and Connectivity**: The design of future Lenovo laptops will likely focus on user ergonomics, incorporating adjustable keyboards and touchpads that provide enhanced comfort during prolonged usage. Additionally, with the increase in remote collaboration, we can expect innovations in connectivity features, such as integrated 5G capabilities and advanced Wi-Fi 6E support, ensuring users stay connected at all times.

Sustainability and Eco-Friendly Initiatives

As environmental concerns grow, Lenovo is making strides toward sustainability, which is likely to shape the future of its laptop offerings.

- **Eco-Friendly Materials**: Lenovo is committed to incorporating more recycled and eco-friendly materials in its products. Future laptops may utilise sustainable plastics and other materials that minimise environmental impact while maintaining high performance standards.
- **Energy Efficiency**: The development of energy-efficient components will be a priority, with Lenovo aiming to reduce the

carbon footprint of its laptops. This could involve the integration of low-power processors and optimised thermal management systems that allow devices to operate effectively without excessive energy consumption.

Predictions for the Next Generation of Lenovo Laptops

As we look ahead, several predictions can be made regarding the next generation of Lenovo laptops:

- **Greater Customization Options**: Future models may offer increased customization capabilities, allowing users to tailor their laptops to better suit their needs. This could include modular components that can be upgraded or replaced, enabling users to enhance performance without needing to invest in entirely new devices.
- **Immersive Experiences**: Lenovo is expected to enhance the multimedia experience on its laptops through

improvements in display technology. This may include higher resolution screens, improved colour accuracy, and the integration of OLED technology, making content consumption and creative tasks more enjoyable.

- **Integration of Mixed Reality**: As mixed reality technologies become more prevalent, Lenovo could lead the way in integrating such features into their laptops. This may involve the incorporation of advanced cameras and sensors that enable augmented reality experiences, further blurring the lines between digital and physical environments.

Glossary of Terms

A

- **AI (Artificial Intelligence)**: Technology that enables machines to perform tasks that typically require human intelligence.
- **AMD (Advanced Micro Devices)**: A company that produces processors and GPUs used in many laptops.
- **APU (Accelerated Processing Unit)**: A type of processor that combines both CPU and GPU functionalities.

B

- **BIOS (Basic Input/Output System)**: Firmware used to perform hardware initialization during the booting process.

- **Battery Life**: Duration a laptop can operate on a single charge.

C

- **CPU (Central Processing Unit)**: The primary component that performs most of the processing inside a laptop.
- **Cortex**: A series of CPU architectures developed by ARM Holdings.

D

- **Display**: The screen of a laptop, which can vary in size and technology (e.g., LCD, OLED).
- **Docking Station**: A device that allows a laptop to connect to multiple peripherals easily.

E

- **Ethernet**: A wired network technology used for local area networks.

- **eGPU (External Graphics Processing Unit)**: A device that connects to a laptop to enhance its graphics performance.

F

- **Firmware**: Software programmed into the hardware of a laptop, enabling it to operate.
- **FHD (Full High Definition)**: A display resolution of 1920x1080 pixels.

G

- **GPU (Graphics Processing Unit)**: A specialised processor designed to accelerate graphics rendering.
- **Graphics Card**: A hardware component that processes and renders images.

H

- **HDMI (High-Definition Multimedia Interface)**: A connection standard for transmitting audio and video data.

- **Hertz**: A measure of frequency that indicates how many cycles per second a processor can perform.

I

- **I/O Ports**: Input/Output ports for connecting peripherals and devices to a laptop.
- **Integrated Graphics**: Graphics processing capability built into the CPU, rather than a separate GPU.

J

- **Jargon**: Specialised terminology used in a particular field, such as technology.

K

- **Kbps (Kilobits per second)**: A measure of data transfer speed.

L

- **LAN (Local Area Network)**: A network that connects computers within a limited area.
- **Linux**: An open-source operating system used in various computing devices, including some Lenovo laptops.

M

- **Machine Learning**: A subset of AI that focuses on the development of algorithms that allow computers to learn from data.
- **M.2**: A type of connector used for SSDs and other devices.

N

- **NVIDIA**: A company known for producing high-performance GPUs used in gaming and professional laptops.
- **NAT (Network Address Translation)**: A technique used to remap one IP address space into another.

O

- **Operating System (OS)**: Software that manages computer hardware and software resources; examples include Windows and Linux.
- **OLED (Organic Light Emitting Diode)**: A display technology that offers better contrast and colour than traditional LCDs.

P

- **Portability**: The ease with which a laptop can be transported and used in various locations.
- **Processor**: Another term for CPU, responsible for executing instructions and processing data.

Q

- **Quad-Core**: A CPU architecture with four cores for improved multitasking and performance.

R

- **RAM (Random Access Memory)**: Memory used by a computer to store data temporarily for quick access.
- **Resolution**: The number of pixels displayed on the screen, affecting image clarity.

S

- **SSD (Solid State Drive)**: A storage device that uses flash memory for faster data access than traditional hard drives.
- **Thunderbolt**: A hardware interface that allows the connection of external peripherals to a laptop.

T

- **Thermal Management**: Techniques used to control the temperature of a laptop's components.
- **Trackpad**: A touch-sensitive surface used for cursor control.

U

- **USB (Universal Serial Bus)**: A standard for connecting devices and transferring data.
- **UHD (Ultra High Definition)**: A display resolution of 3840x2160 pixels.

V

- **Virtualization**: The creation of virtual versions of physical components, such as servers or storage devices.
- **VPN (Virtual Private Network)**: A technology that creates a secure connection over the internet.

W

- **Wi-Fi**: A technology for wireless networking that enables devices to connect to the internet.
- **Windows**: A popular operating system developed by Microsoft.

X

- **XLR**: A type of electrical connector used for audio and video equipment, though not common in laptops.

Y

- **YouTube**: A video-sharing platform often used for tech tutorials and reviews.

Z

- **Zoom**: A video conferencing tool that has gained popularity for remote work and meetings.

www.ingramcontent.com/pod-product-compliance
Lightning Source LLC
LaVergne TN
LVHW051741050326
832903LV00029B/2656